£14.99

The Asperger Children's Toolkit

Francis Musgrave

First published in 2012
by Jessica Kingsley Publishers
116 Pentonville Road
London N1 9JB, UK
and
400 Market Street, Suite 400
Philadelphia, PA 19106, USA

www.jkp.com

Copyright © Francis Musgrave 2012

Library of Congress Cataloging in Publication Data
A CIP catalog record for this book is available from the Library of Congress

British Library Cataloguing in Publication Data
A CIP catalogue record for this book is available from the British Library

ISBN 978 1 84905 293 1

Printed and bound in China

I dedicate this book to my wife and daughter.
Together they have pushed back the boundaries
and limitations of common convention, and
refused to accept the dogma of others.
I'm proud to be a member of their team.

Contents

Introduction for Parents

The Asperger Children's Toolkit is packed full of fun and practical ideas to help you and your child work through the challenges of Asperger Syndrome (AS).

The book takes a positive view about what these challenges are and how they might be dealt with on a day-to-day basis from your child's perspective.

Children with AS face many day-to-day experiences that to others might seem uneventful; to them these are anything but.

It's particularly important to work with your child as a team, to help him or her understand both that their burden is shared and that you have a collective responsibility to collaborate with them to help them find solutions.

Many might argue that this is surely what parenthood is about anyway. While I would not disagree, the intensity and scope of parental involvement is particularly important in supporting children with AS, and is only achieved by constant positive reinforcement, and engagement through play and other enjoyable learning experiences.

Why The Asperger Children's Toolkit?

As a family that deals with the consequences of AS every day, we believe that no child or parent/carer should have to undergo the anxiety and pain we endured on our road to discovering what AS was, and how to deal with it.

As we travelled our particular road we have been fortunate enough to meet many children, families and other experts who have shared their experiences and insights into AS with us.

This book represents the distillation of our collective acquired knowledge, which has been reshaped into a format that can be used repeatedly on a day-to-day basis.

It's designed to help children aged approximately 8–12 to discover things about themselves that will help them in their home and wider environments. By both understanding and overcoming difficulties alongside your child, you can meet these challenges together as a team, which will make them seem less daunting and appear far more achievable. This will help to build a track record of success that is so vital both for shaping your child's view of the world and for giving them the confidence they need not just to survive, but to thrive.

This book deliberately does not talk about boundaries or discipline, but focuses instead on understanding and reinforcing positive behaviour.

About this Book

This book uses some very simple principles that we call the 'AS Active Approach'. Easily understood, they are designed to be implemented and maintained against the backdrop of the constant drip-feed of new obstacles that make up the everyday lives of a family living with the challenges of AS.

While we can only ever hope to 'do our best', doing our best requires an investment of time and effort that will pay dividends if sustained and will manifest itself in a happier, more fulfilling relationship with your child.

These key principles are:

1. Understanding the underlying causes of problems rather than simply the symptoms, and being prepared to deal with detail.

2. Using praise rather than punishment to reinforce good behaviour.

3. Formulating positive 'win/win' alternative ways of dealing with problems; and being creative, especially when emotions are running high.

4. Building a collaborative team between child, parents and carers, family and educators.

5. Developing diplomacy, and dealing with delay and disappointment.

6. Looking after yourself and allowing time for respite, recovery and reset.

About the AS Active Approach

It's a collection of ideas and principles

Put simply, AS Active is an approach which emphasises the importance of collaboration to improve the quality of everyone's lives. It has four basic principles:

★ *Working together as a team:* with parents, carers, family members and educators on a series of activities that allow you to monitor progress, build on success and learn from the outcomes. There is no such thing as failure in the AS Active principle, only learning.

★ *Building on success:* even the very smallest of successes need to be recognised, applauded and rewarded if possible. When things don't go according to plan, or don't have the outcome you expected, it's important to see these for what they are too. Not a reason for anger, sadness or frustration, but a turning point in knowledge and understanding. Because without understanding how would any of us know how to change anything for the better?

★ *Having fun together:* with every job that's to be done, there really can be an element of fun. It's all about how we approach what we do. People who are good at what they do tend to enjoy what they do, and what they do can often bring joy to others. This approach can also be used to resolve problems, relieve tensions and focus our energies on what really matters. Because pleasure lowers the barriers to learning, understanding and acceptance, so is a very powerful tool.

★ *Refresh and renewal:* a good diet, exercise and sleep are clearly important for us all. But even more so for AS Active parents, carers and children. The physical and emotional toll that having a stressful life takes on anyone cannot be underestimated so it's vital that people take some time for themselves to come away from the coal face for a while, reconnect to the world, and put everything back into perspective.

Although much of this book is based on the well-trodden path of experience, it's also about learning and having fun together as a team with an emotional bond and a common purpose. If we play together, we'll stay together and enrich each other's lives. For more information about AS Active visit us at: www.asactive.org.

Why is the AS Active Approach so Important?

★ Mammalian brains have 'plasticity', a natural mechanism designed by nature to learn and adapt behaviours relevant to a living environment, or environmental changes. This is a key aid to survival.

★ In humans this brain function is highly developed, and normally it is particularly flexible in children.

★ Neurotypical children tend to adapt intuitively, but children with AS need to learn to adapt as an active process, because they cannot always link cause and effect in the way their peers do.

★ By forming new associative pathways and new behaviour patterns we are in effect reshaping or helping to rewire the brain.

★ Play is a particularly effective way of doing this as it removes many of the processing barriers because it is an enjoyable experience.

★ This is why AS Active uses the strap line 'Play–Learn–Connect'.

★ It's a simple idea, with remarkable benefits.

An Overview of Asperger Syndrome

★ Children with AS may have many different presentations. Every child is different, so one size does not fit all. Sometimes even the same thing doesn't work twice.

★ Anxiety and the desire to socialise are inextricably linked, so help your child learn how to solve social problems, and learn from those experiences both good and bad.

★ Children with AS often have difficulty with implementing theory into practice, so constant exposure and repetition is key.

★ Social play needs to be guided and interesting, but most of all, fun.

★ Praise and reward often, never be negative – it's about guidance, not discipline.

★ We are all learning together, so don't be afraid to try new things.

★ What you do isn't easy, but it makes a big difference.

Understanding Asperger Syndrome

★ AS was discovered by Dr Hans Asperger working in Austria in 1944.

★ AS is a lifelong condition that allows you to see the world differently from others, and is part of the Autistic Spectrum.

★ 'Autism' is derived from the Greek word *autos*, which means 'self'. It alludes to one of the most dominant aspects of the condition: the challenge inherent in empathising with or understanding others.

★ The word 'spectrum' is used because, while people with autism may share similar areas of difficulty, these challenges will affect them in very different ways.

The Challenges of Asperger Syndrome

Sometimes it can seem like a tough challenge...

...but by taking a positive approach, overcoming setbacks, and working closely with your parents as a team, in time you'll learn that nothing can hold you back from reaching your goals.

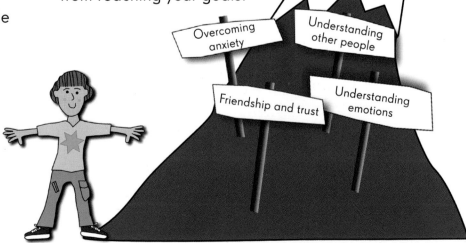

Overcoming anxiety

Understanding other people

Friendship and trust

Understanding emotions

Some Cool Things about Asperger Syndrome

★ The Asperger mind tends to be a specialist mind, and can often be good at certain things, but not all children with AS have exceptional gifts of the kind that are reported.

★ Most children with AS respond well to visual stimulation. This is because much of their thinking is centred around the primary visual cortex, the part of the brain that processes visual information.

★ Children with AS can often have highly developed patterns of thinking:

　○ *Visual thinkers* may have difficulty with conceptual or purely theoretical ideas, but make wonderful artists and designers.

　○ *Pattern thinkers* might be musical, mathematical or engineering type minds.

　○ *Verbal thinkers* are usually highly articulate and able to recall a vast array of factual information.

★ Bright children with AS are often described as 'little professors'.

Sensory Issues

Some children with AS may have issues with processing sensory input in a meaningful way. They may be oversensitive or undersensitive to different types of stimuli, for example:

★ visual – pictures on TV, brightness/darkness

★ auditory – loud noises, a certain pitch

★ vestibular – balance and shifting position

★ olfactory – smells (often oversensitive, smelling things that others cannot)

★ gustatory – taste, certain foods (often linked with smell)

★ proprioceptive – stimuli from within the body itself, especially those related to muscle states or movement.

Sensory overload is common. If it all gets too much it can lead to a Meltdown.

What's a Meltdown?

Meltdowns can be caused by many things, such as:

★ anxiety

★ a response to a disagreeable event or conversation

★ a response to sensory overload

★ the frustration of not being able or allowed to express emotions.

What form can they take?

★ Repetitive behaviour, rocking to and fro.

★ Curling up in a ball.

★ Hiding under a table or desk.

★ Aggressive behaviour.

★ Appearing withdrawn and uncommunicative.

★ Covering the head with hair or hands, or indeed anything.

Dealing with meltdowns

All parents and children have their own techniques for dealing with meltdowns. Here are some common ones:

★ Cuddling/deep compression (a tight hug or squeeze).

★ Sensory exclusion (e.g. covering with a blanket).

★ Talking (cognitive or talking therapy).

★ Distraction/redirection.

AS Activities

The following activities will help you understand more about AS.

It's important to recognise that AS exists in your life, and to work through the challenges that it presents together with your parents and teachers.

The activities are designed to help you and others around you to understand what AS is and how to shrink the negative parts of it, and to grow the positive parts.

These activities are designed to make you think, and develop your own unique solutions with those you care about, and who care about you.

The Brain Guru
It's all about self-help

Welcome to the art of self-help

Perfected over many thousands of years, what you will learn really is life-changing.

But remember, this is a journey, not a destination. Your destination is what you choose it to be, and your journey will help you learn to make the right choices.

Every journey starts with a single step.

So let's begin.

Understanding Your Mind Requires that You Understand its Relationship with Your Body

Your mind and your body are linked by the nervous system.

Did you know that you can change the way your mind interprets the signals it receives from your body, as well as sending it powerful messages?

This idea is as old as humankind.

Try these amazing mind control methods

1 **An antidote to stress.** Regular physical exercise produces adrenalin in your bloodstream and this acts as a natural antidote to stress. But don't overdo it. Like everything in life, it needs to be balanced.

2 **Feeling anxious?** Blow on the back of your hand, using long, deep puffs. The vagus nerve that controls the speed at which your heart pumps is slowed down by the rate of your breathing. The air rushing across the back of your hand also has a cooling and soothing **effect**.

3 **Feeling nervous?** Try a firm cuddle from a parent or a friend. This deep compression stimulates many nerve endings at once and helps the brain to become settled and calm.

4 **Worried about something?** Place your index finger in front of your eyes at arm's length. Move it from left to right while following it with your eyes, without moving your head. Your eye movement will help your brain re-synchronise what it knows with what it feels. This is quite a new discovery, and scientists aren't quite sure why it works, just that it does.

From Small Seeds Grow Big Oak Trees

Growing anything starts with planting the seed of an idea.

If you feed your idea, over time it will grow in size and strength.

Even seedlings struggle in the first few days, it's as if the whole earth is pushing against them. But in time not even this can hold them back.

This idea is as old as time itself.

6 Over time, take a moment with a parent to congratulate yourself on how well you have done.

I'll do more trips to the same place

5 Work through the tree ideas gradually, ticking off your achievements with a big red pen.

I'll start going to different places nearby

4 Start with small leaves, and expand your idea gradually; the bigger the step, the bigger the leaf.

I'll start with a short trip

Growing your own thought tree

3 Use string or wool to link each leaf.

2 Simply write what you want to do on your 'seed of an idea', and stick it to your wall near the floor.

1 Cut out the leaves and seeds from the following page.

I can go shopping whenever I want

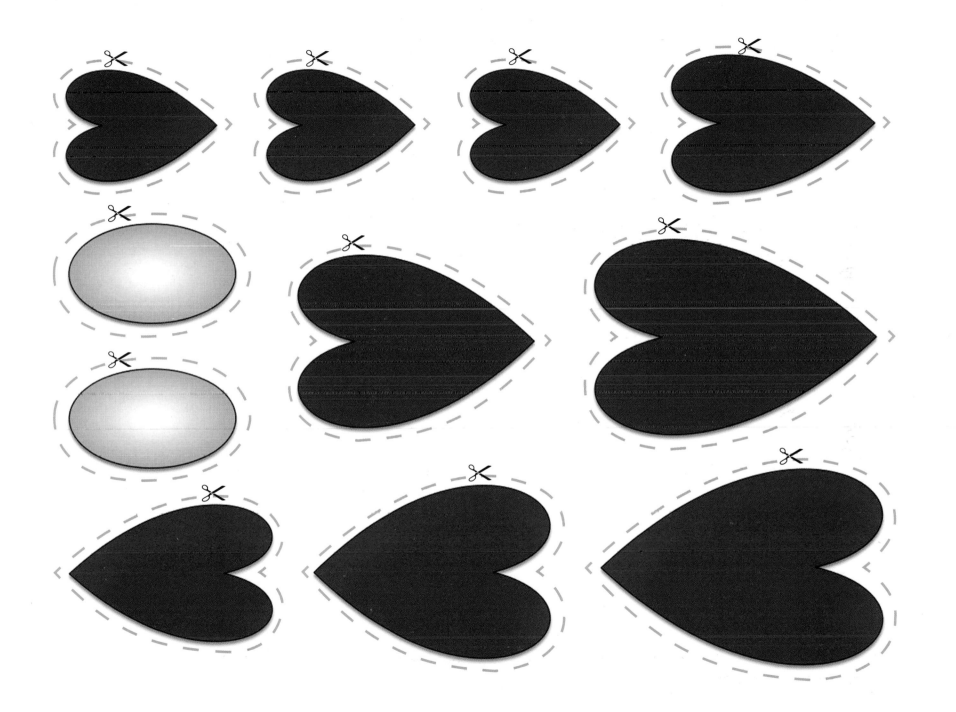

Removing Unwanted and Negative Thoughts

Understanding how unlikely or unreal a negative thought is will help give you more fun and happiness.

This idea is very simple, but incredibly powerful. Use it wisely.

How to use it ✂

1. Cut out, fold and glue or tape the 'Thinking Out of the Box' box.

2. Cut out the thought clouds, and with a parent discuss and label the clouds by writing the cause of the anxiety on each cloud.

3. It may help to fold the clouds slightly, to make them easier to pick up later.

4. Put the clouds in the box, cover it with your hand and give it a good shake.

5. Remove each cloud one by one and talk with your parent about how *you* would solve that particular problem.

6. Only when you have agreed on a workable solution can the cloud be destroyed.

Don't be afraid to put a cloud back into the box if a problem is difficult to solve – you can always come back to it later.

This principle can be used for both general and specific anxieties, but it's important to have the discussion in a calm and positive way.

Thinking Out of the Box

Thinking Out of the Box

Thinking Out of the Box

Thinking Out of the Box

Learning to Take Charge of Your Thoughts and Emotions

This can actually help to:

★ make you smarter

★ reduce your anxiety

★ get rid of negative thoughts.

This idea is over 1000 years old, so I guess it must work pretty well.

The Brain Guru is pretty wise (he's old and experienced), so there isn't much he doesn't know about how to control mind and body.
Try this for yourself, it's pretty amazing. Ask a parent to help or do it with you.

5

4

3

2

1

1 In a quiet room, sit on the floor with your back to a wall.

2 Close your eyes and breathe deeply in and out for about five seconds.

3 Keeping your eyes closed, relax your muscles, and think about the best thing you've ever done and nothing else. Remember it like it was yesterday.

4 Hold your thoughts for as long as you can. Talk about it if it helps; then open your eyes when you are ready.

5 Do this every day, and you too may one day be the master of your thoughts, and be a Brain Guru too.

You Have Come Far on Your Journey

Let us take a moment to review your mastery of the Brain Guru tools and techniques

See how your confidence grows as you use these techniques.

Week 1　Week 2　Week 3　Week 4

Remember, anything worth doing takes time to achieve.

Black Belt
Mastery of all four challenges

Brown Belt
Mastery of three challenges

Green Belt
Mastery of two challenges

Orange Belt
Mastery of a single challenge

White Belt
Has begun their journey

Catalogue of Success

It's all about building on successful experiences

Having a Catalogue of Success is a great way to boost your self-confidence, and show you just how far you've come and what you've achieved.

Being able to look back at your successes is a great way to put some of the more difficult days into perspective too. The Catalogue of Success can be done daily, weekly, or however often works for you.

The best bit is they are really easy to make. Here's how:

Your Catalogue of Success

Working through a tough day

Even though you were anxious, you went to school, went to see the doctor with your mum in the afternoon, and still made time to attend soccer class in the evening.

What a long and busy day – this took real guts and determination. You should be proud of yourself and of your achievements. Well done!

Fantastic social interaction

You are one brave girl! You played and chatted beautifully with Samantha.

You did not give in to your anxiety – this shows you are in control of your thoughts and your life, you know who you are and what you want. You are awesome.

Meeting new people

You met a new person on Tuesday, and you were very kind and courteous, and very brave in talking with her. You did not let your anxiety control you – you controlled your anxiety. Even though you thought it was strange, you had a go at the emotional freedom techniques that we learnt from the Brain Guru.

This shows that you have the confidence to try new things. You have the power to overcome any problem you encounter. Well done!

Sharing and caring

You taught your younger sister Jane how to play your Ukulele.

You shared your things, and took the time and trouble to teach your sister a new skill. Best of all, you and Jane had fun together. You are a kind, loving, gentle and very unique person. Thank you for enriching everyone's lives.

1. Make a list of categories of achievement (see the example list headings on the following page for ideas), leaving space under each heading to add details about things that have gone well or what you have achieved.

2. Add these details under each heading. Write about what's gone well and highlight the skill or character trait that helped bring about that success. If things haven't gone as well as you'd hoped, focus on what you've learned.

3. Add some photos or pictures to help you remember what you felt like at the time.

4. Keep your pages in a folder in a safe place, and make sure you review them frequently, particularly when you are feeling sad or low.

You'll soon have a huge Catalogue of Success that will help build your self-confidence and show you that you can achieve anything if you put your mind to it.

Your Catalogue of Success

Here is an example

List heading

The achievement

Working through a tough day

Even though you were anxious, you went to school, went to see the doctor with your mum in the afternoon, and still made time to attend soccer class in the evening.

What a long and busy day – this took real guts and determination. You should be proud of yourself and of your achievements. Well done!

What this shows us about you and the wonderful things you can do

Fantastic social interaction

You are one brave girl! You played and chatted beautifully with Samantha.

You did not give in to your anxiety – this shows you are in control of your thoughts and your life, you know who you are and what you want. You are awesome.

Meeting new people

You met a new person on Tuesday, and you were very kind and courteous, and very brave in talking with her. You did not let your anxiety control you – you controlled your anxiety. Even though you thought it was strange, you had a go at the emotional freedom techniques that we learnt from the Brain Guru.

This shows that you have the confidence to try new things. You have the power to overcome any problem you encounter. Well done!

Sharing and caring

You taught your younger sister Jane how to play your Ukulele.

You shared your things, and took the time and trouble to teach your sister a new skill. Best of all, you and Jane had fun together. You are a kind, loving, gentle and very unique person. Thank you for enriching everyone's lives.

The Sensory Detective
It's all about self-discovery and problem solving

Welcome to the science of self-discovery and problem solving

Perfected over many years, what you will learn really is life-changing.

It will help you discover things about yourself that in turn will help you to make the right choices and overcome many of the difficulties you face.

To solve any mystery you need to gather evidence, understand motives, and see opportunities.

But remember, behind every successful detective there is a hard-working team.

So let's begin.

Just Like a Computer, Your Brain Collects and Processes Information 24 Hours a Day

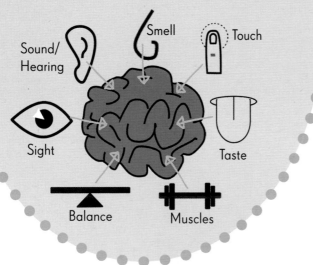

Your brain and your body are linked by the nervous system, the network of cables that picks up signals of touch, taste, smell, sound and sight, as well as balance and your own body's muscle movements.

Smell
Touch
Sound/ Hearing
Sight
Taste
Balance
Muscles

When you encounter something you don't like, your brain makes one of three very quick decisions about what to do.

These are called 'behavioural responses', and sometimes they can get you into trouble with your family, friends and teachers, if they don't understand what you are feeling and why.

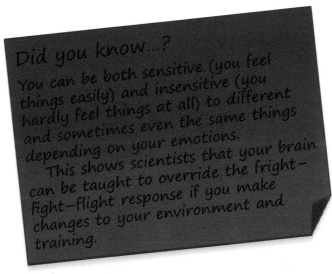

Did you know....?

You can be both sensitive (you feel things easily) and insensitive (you hardly feel things at all) to different and sometimes even the same things depending on your emotions.

This shows scientists that your brain can be taught to override the fright–fight–flight response if you make changes to your environment and training.

Fright
Being very scared or anxious.

Fight
Wanting to fight or push it away.

Flight
Wanting to get away as quickly as possible.

As All Good Detectives Know, the Next Step is to Gather Evidence

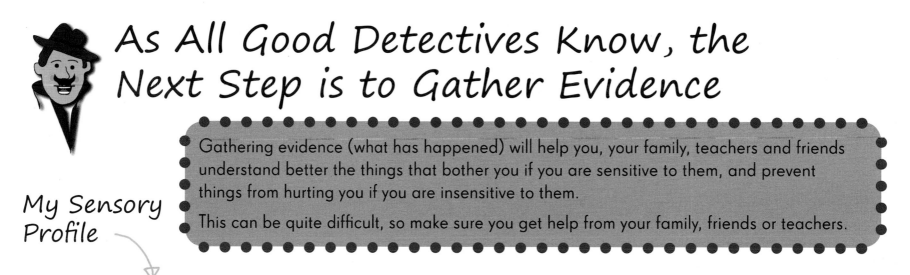

Gathering evidence (what has happened) will help you, your family, teachers and friends understand better the things that bother you if you are sensitive to them, and prevent things from hurting you if you are insensitive to them.

This can be quite difficult, so make sure you get help from your family, friends or teachers.

My Sensory Profile

Sense	When I...	What happens is...	It feels like...	What could *we* do about it?
Sight				
Sound/Hearing				
Touch				
Smell				
Taste				
Balance				
Muscle movement				

For example:				
In 'Touch' you might write:	Have a shower	I feel uncomfortable	My skin hurts	I could have a bath instead
In 'Muscle movement' you might write:	Am walking	I often bump into things	There is no real sensation	We could do some sensitivity training

29

Small Changes Can Make a Big Difference

By making small changes to what you do and how you think about them, you can make big changes to the enjoyment of your own life and those around you.

Here are some simple examples to get you started, I'm sure *you* can think of lots more.

Remember, it can often be more than one thing that makes you feel the need for the fright, fight or flight behavioural response.

Evidence (what happens?)	Motive (why?)	Opportunity (for you and others to help solve the problem!)
Do people comment that you are not making eye contact during conversation?	You may be uncomfortable with direct visual attention to another person's face because you may have difficulty processing facial expressions or body language.	Ask your parent/carer to provide you with a sound and sight cue to direct your attention. For example, they could use their finger to gesture while saying 'Look at me'. Or you could imagine a fixed point on someone's face and look at it while speaking to them.
Do you often get told to keep your hands and feet to yourself while sitting in a group?	It might be that you want tactile (touch) input, or you may have difficulty understanding personal boundaries.	Ask your parent/carer to provide a cue for personal boundaries, such as a mat or cushion to sit on, and ask them to get you a fidget item such as a tangle or small stress ball.
Do you not like brushing your teeth?	It could be because the brush bristles are too hard and irritating, or the toothpaste tastes disgusting.	Ask your parent/carer to get you a softer toothbrush. Try different toothpaste flavours, or even how you put the toothpaste on the brush. Try dipping the brush in toothpaste rather than putting a blob on the brush.
Do you get very anxious in the dining room or cafeteria?	Loud echos, lots of movement and strong smells might be causing you stress.	You could ask your teacher to let you go to the lunch room early, or allow you to eat in the classroom. Get your parent/carer to make you your favourite sandwiches. Or go into the lunch room with an adult or older student you trust to help you if you have problems.
Do you dislike or feel uncomfortable in certain clothes?	You may have what scientists call a 'tactile hypersensitivity' to certain materials when they are placed on your body. This is very common indeed, lots of people have it.	Try lots of different clothes with your parent/carer to find out what you are most comfortable in. Sometimes you can de-sensitise some of your feelings towards some materials by getting your parent/carer to give you a massage or a firm rub with a towel over a period of time. Oh, and ask them to remove clothing tags if they irritate you.
Do you find that some smells, tastes or textures of some foods make you feel uncomfortable or sick?	Did you know that much of what you think you taste, you actually smell? But you can have a hypersensitivity to almost any sense.	Ask your parent/carer not to give you foods you don't like. You could try pinching your nose to close your nostrils when you eat. Or try very small portions of certain foods to see if you can de-sensitise yourself to them.
Do you have trouble carrying liquids without spilling them?	You may have difficulty in judging body position and balance.	Try increasing the weight of the container and reduce the level of its content. For example, use a heavier beaker and fill it only half full.

The Sensory Feel-o-Meter

To understand
if these changes are
making things better or worse,
we need to get 'feedback' from *you*.

Feedback tells parents and carers to do
more, or less, or even to stop if necessary.

It could be that you have encountered something
we didn't know about, so you need to tell us.

To help others understand
how you feel about things,
here's how to use the meter:

High – I'm very uncomfortable.
Slow down or STOP.

Just right – I'm comfortable now.

Low – I'm feeling low,
let's do something.

Ask your parent and carer or teacher
to help you cut out and put together
the Sensory Feel-o-Meter™.

✂

The Sensory Feel-o-Meter™

Just Right

Low

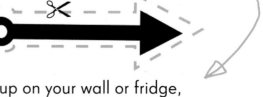

Put it up on your wall or fridge,
and use it to tell people about
how you are feeling.

Opportunities: Sensory Fun and Games

You can actually have a lot of fun with your senses.

What's even better is, every time you try something new and then repeat it, your brain slightly changes its reaction to it.

So with practice you can completely change how you feel about something.

Making a human sausage roll

Use a blanket or rug and ask a family member to roll you in it.

How does it help?
The snug, cosy feeling that it gives you (often, but not always) will help give you a sensation of wellbeing and is very calming, particularly if you feel stressed or anxious.

Building a sensory agility course

Using household items, get your family to help you build a sensory agility course.

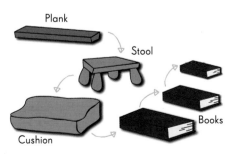

Plank

Stool

Books

Cushion

How does it help?
This helps with balance and coordination of muscle movement (so-called 'motor planning').

It also helps you to adjust sensory messages to your overall nervous system, improving your alertness and agility.

Happy feet

1. Cut out the feet pictures from the next six pages and lay them on the floor.

2. Position them to where you want them to be and use sticky tape to make sure they do not move.

3. See if you can match your feet to the pattern you've laid out.

How does it help?
This is particularly good for balance and coordination of muscle movement.

You could add this to your sensory agility course.

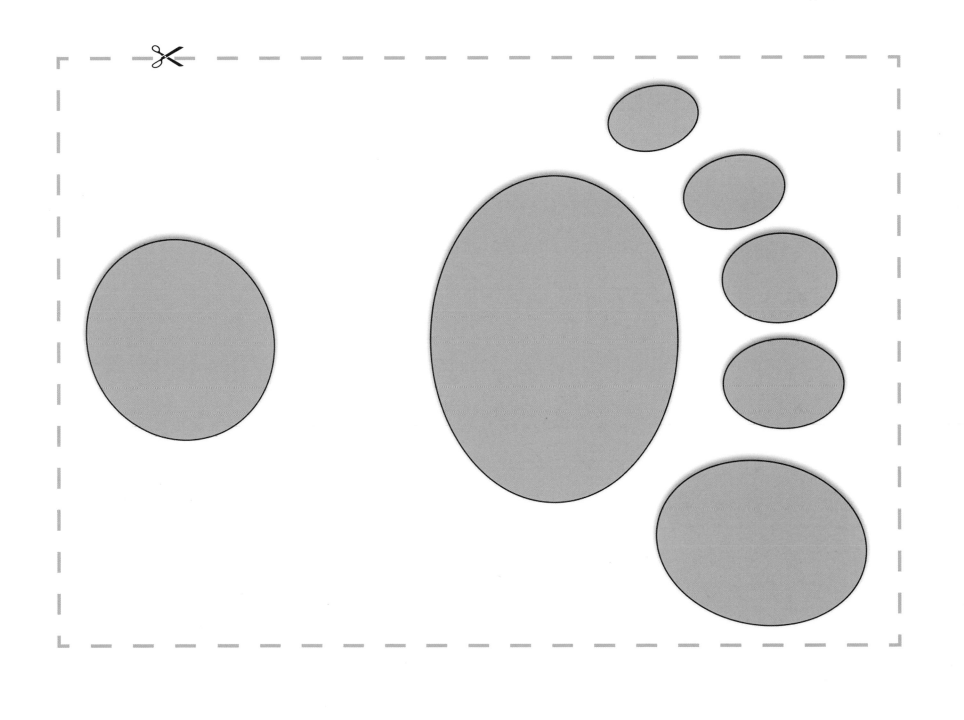

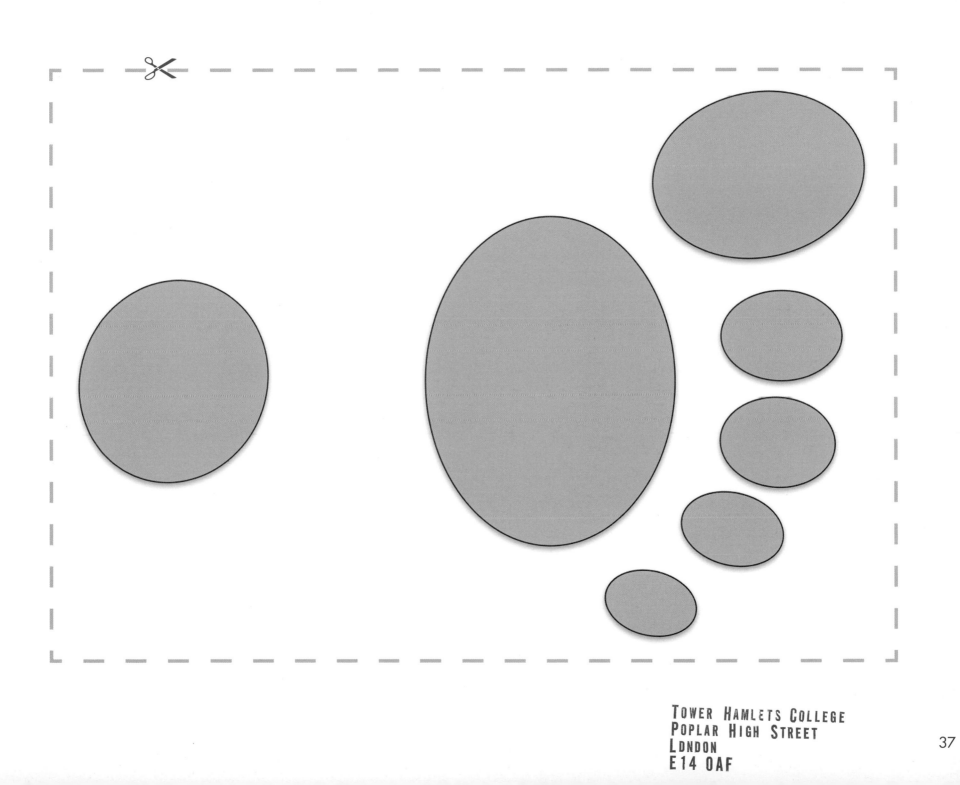

TOWER HAMLETS COLLEGE
POPLAR HIGH STREET
LONDON
E14 0AF

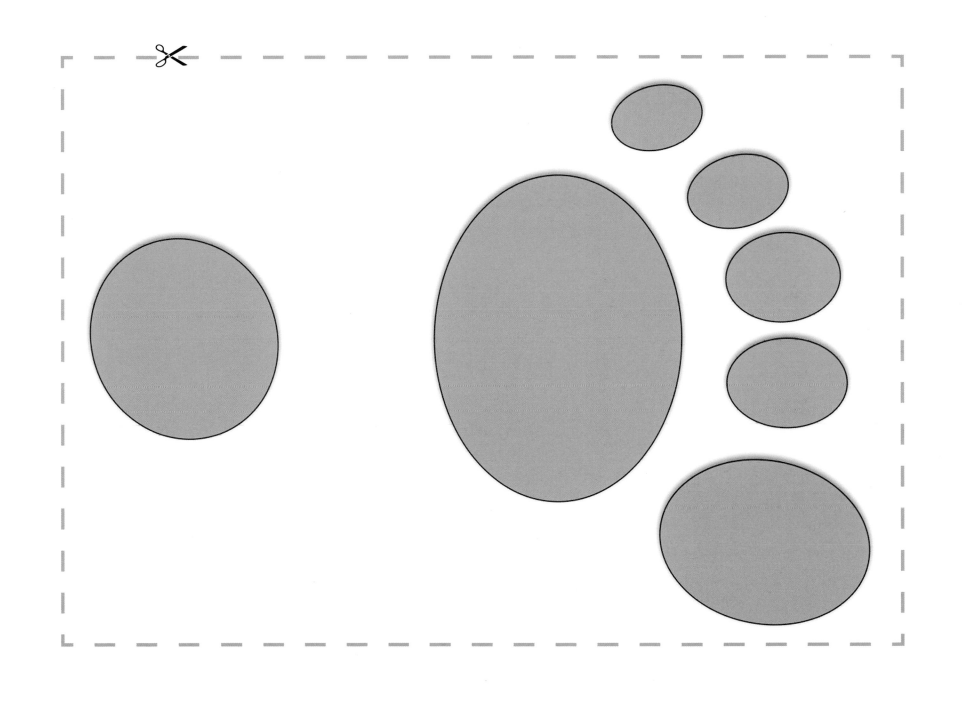

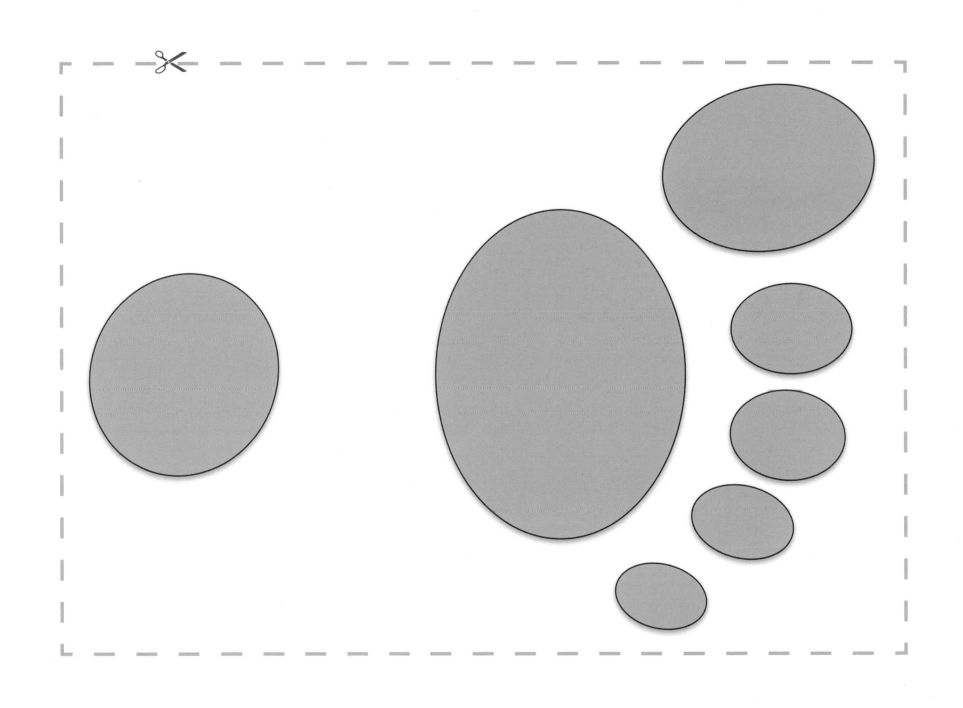

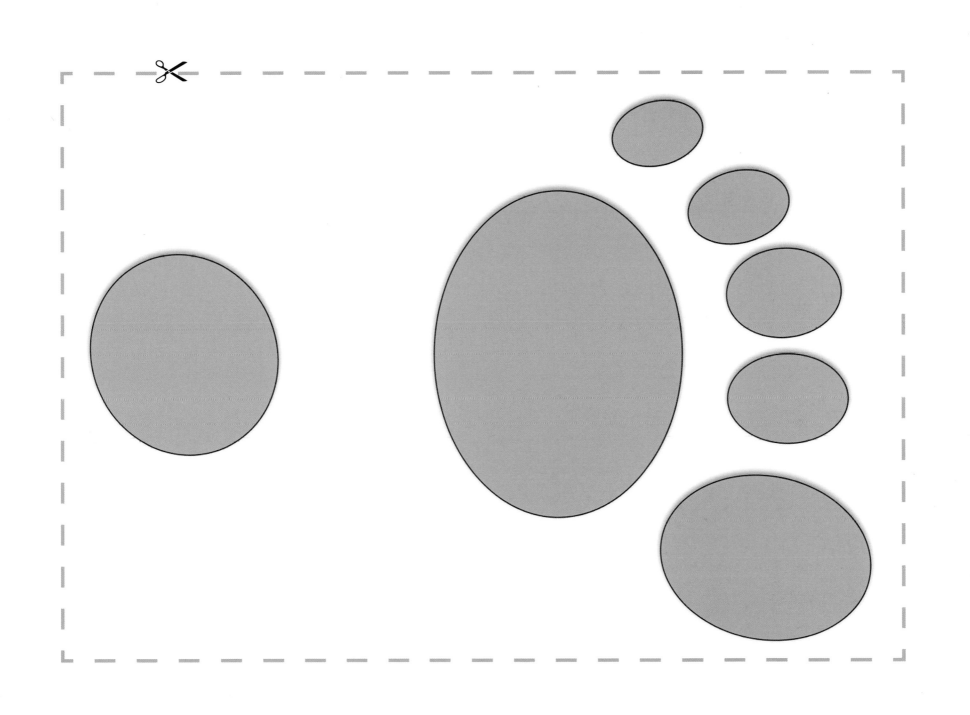

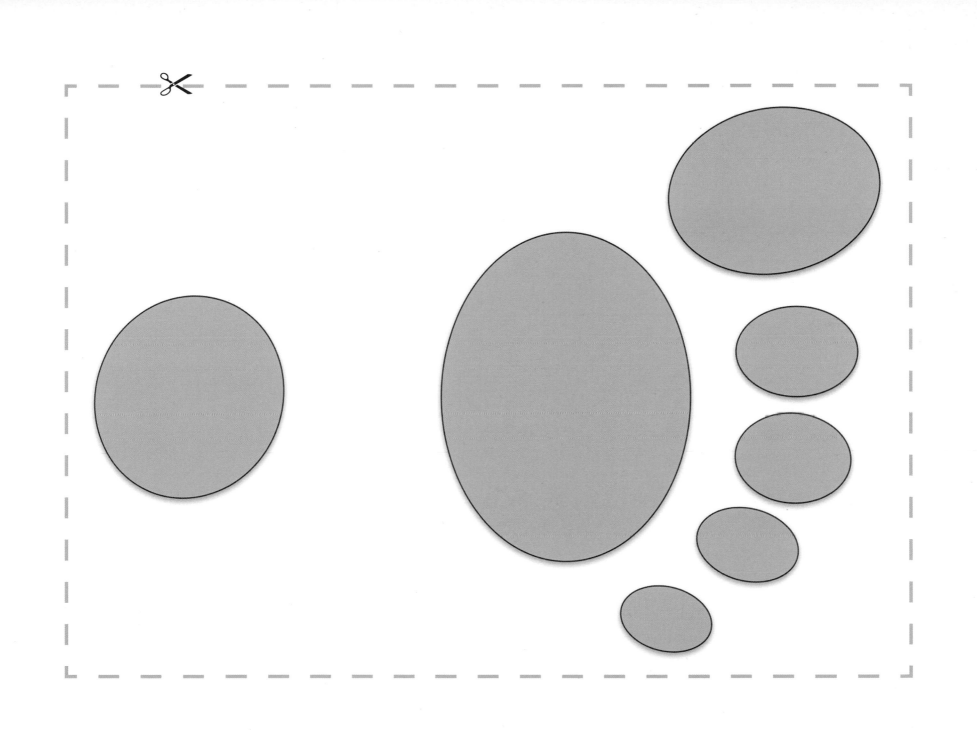

More Opportunities: Sensory Fun and Games

By blocking out some of your senses you can have fun understanding how your brain copes.

The visual sensory mask

1. Cut out the mask and make two holes where the two dots are.

2. Use elastic or wool as a strap to hold the mask to your face.

3. You now have a blindfold, so let's see if we can fool your senses!

Is it smell or is it taste?

4. While you are wearing the mask and cannot see, ask a friend or family member to make you two cold drinks to approximately the same strength. For example, one could be blackcurrant cordial, and the other might be orange squash.

5. Pinching your nose tightly, taste each drink (no peeking!), and see if you can tell them apart.

   Try it with food of a similar texture too. Generally, the stronger the smell, the more difficult it is to tell the difference.

No sight or sound, just touch

6. While you are wearing the mask and cannot see, ask a friend or family member to put some headphones on you that are playing your favourite music (not too loudly).

7. Get them to gently rub different textures across the back of your arm, and see if you can guess what they are.

Visual Sensory Mask

The Social Scientist

It's all about understanding who you are

Welcome to the science of human interaction

Perfected over many generations, what you will learn really is life-changing.

It will help you discover things about yourself and about other people and can really help you and those around you to have a happier life.

Every scientific discovery starts with an examination of what we know.

So let's begin.

Understanding Yourself will Help You to Understand Others

To interact with other human beings we use both our *inner intelligence* and *outer intelligence*.

Understanding yourself is the key to unlocking what can sometimes seem like the mystery of others.

Fundamentally everyone is made up of the same stuff, but how this stuff is mixed together can vary dramatically. This determines our personality, and *everyone* has a *different* personality.

When people get on well together, it's said 'they have good chemistry'.

Like any chemical reaction, if you want a fizz or a bang, it's what you put into the mixture that will determine the type of reaction you get.

Inner intelligence

★ What we know about ourselves.

★ What excites us or makes us sad.

★ What we like and dislike.

★ How we feel about things.

Outer intelligence

★ How we read the reactions of other people.

★ What makes others excited and sad.

★ What others like and dislike.

★ How they feel about things.

Inner Intelligence: Understanding What You Feel

It is sometimes difficult to express how we feel.

If pressure builds up inside you, the result is sudden release, or explosion of emotions.

This can make people around you very nervous, and will not help your relationship with them. Sometimes it can even make matters worse.

It's better to release emotions in a slower, more managed way, so that people can understand better how you feel and how they can help you.

Talking about how you feel is a great place to start: 'A problem shared really is a problem halved.'

The My-Emoto-Meter™ can help you describe to others both what you feel and the intensity of that feeling. It's also a great way for both your inner and outer intelligence to start to work on understanding problems and finding solutions.

Did you know that you lose 30% of your intelligence when you are in an emotional state? Most people would agree you need 100% of your intelligence to solve difficult problems. So being able to manage your emotional state is a very useful skill to learn.

My-Emoto-Meter™

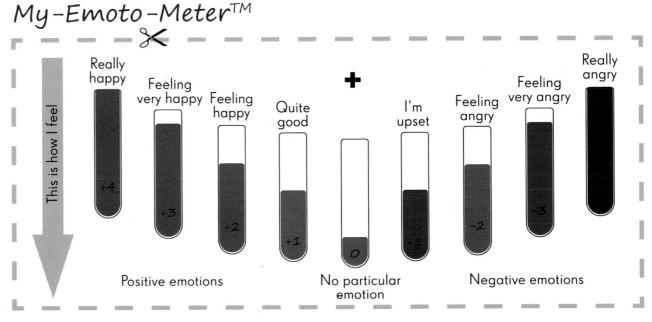

This is how I feel

Really happy +4
Feeling very happy +3
Feeling happy +2
Quite good +1
No particular emotion 0
I'm upset -1
Feeling angry -2
Feeling very angry -3
Really angry

Positive emotions

No particular emotion

Negative emotions

Inner Intelligence: Understanding Why You Feel Emotions

Emotions are part of our survival toolkit. Emotions such as fear help protect us.

Emotions are the body's biochemical response to things that happen to us, and prepare us for what we *think* might happen next. The key word here is '*think*' because we can change what we think by *learning*.

Humans are sophisticated animals, so have a sophisticated set of emotional responses. We can have *simple emotions* like anger or happiness, or *complex emotions* like disappointment or surprise. They are called 'complex' because they change from one state to the other and can often be the most difficult to manage.

Take the weight off your mind

The best way to take the pressure of an emotion off your mind is simply to write it down.

Creating a 'Feelings log' will help you to link *emotions* and *actions*. It's a great way to see what worked and what didn't, and it will also give you the supporting evidence you need for future theories and discoveries about yourself and others. For example:

Date and time	What happened?	How did you feel?	What did you do?	What was the outcome?
	Describe the event as fairly and as accurately as you can. What did you do? What did others do?	How did this make you feel? What physical sensations did you have?	What action did you take?	What happened? Be honest with yourself: 1. Was the outcome good or bad? 2. Would you do the same action again now you know the outcome?

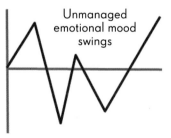

Inner Intelligence: Managing Your Emotions

Managing your emotional state is an important skill to learn.

Without it, you will have difficulty concentrating on your schoolwork, maintaining relationships, and being able to enjoy life.

Remember: everyone has emotions, and successful people tend to be very successful at managing their emotions.

Spikes or curves?

Most people would agree that having rapid changes or spikes of different emotions isn't a good thing. It can make you unpredictable, and the people around you nervous.

Unmanaged emotional mood swings

Everyone has changes in their emotions because of things that happen to us everyday, it's part of being human.

Managed emotional mood swings

The secret is to smooth the spikes into curves, by taking a moment to think about your emotions and how best to deal with them, rather than simply reacting straight away to things that happen to you.

Cause and effect

It's important to know that *any* action you take that involves other people will change in some way how people think about you.

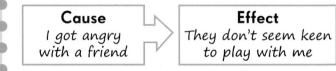

Cause	**Effect**
I got angry with a friend	They don't seem keen to play with me

Generally, positive things have a positive effect on people, while negative things have a negative effect. A good rule is, 'Treat other people how you'd like to be treated yourself.'

Your emotional state

Your attitude to others

Your behaviour towards others

Your relationship with others

Others' attitudes towards you

Others' behaviour towards you

Why managing your emotions is so important

Inner Intelligence: Emotion Tools

A negative emotional journey can often be an unpredictable one, and can often be unpleasant both for you and for those around you.

Here are some really useful tools and techniques you can use to help you regain your emotional balance when you come across a situation that upsets you.

Once you've learned these you can use them over and over again in many situations.

Many of these ideas come from the world of sport, where they help athletes to focus on what's important.

Reframing

1 Take a moment to look at your personal situation. Imagine it as a picture in a frame.

2 Think about the positives:
  ○ how far you have come
  ○ the wonderful things you're going to do and achieve.

Positive things only in this space

3 The negative things that you have to deal with are kept outside this frame and are simply things you have to overcome to reach your goal.

4 Visualize yourself working within this positive framework, focusing on achieving your goals. Keep your eye on the prize, not the things that hold you back.

Visualization

Have you ever wondered what it would feel like to reach your goals, hopes and dreams? Well, visualization is all about just that.

Imagining what 'good' feels, tastes and smells like will help you focus on how to reach your goals, and to set aside things that prevent you from reaching them, like self-doubt, worries and anxiety – as well as people and events that you see as blocking your path or discouraging you.

Someone once said, 'You can do almost anything, if you put your mind to it,' and that is pretty much true. But you need one other thing, and that's a plan. Your plan needs to be realistic and achievable. If it's not, your dreams will remain just that. So start with something small, and as your accomplishments grow, so too can the realisation of your dreams.

When you get sad or angry, use this to remind yourself of your purpose. Any unkind words or actions by others just strengthen your resolve to make your dreams come true.

Pause and reflect

It's often the case that things are not what they seem, and responding too early without thinking things through may actually make matters worse.

Try this idea with people around you that you trust. Often their input (even though you may not always agree with it) will help you to see things in a different way.

When you get angry about someone or something ask yourself three simple questions:

1 Did this event or person intentionally set out to upset or hurt you?

2 What would they have to gain by doing this?

3 How can *you* improve the situation so that it does not get worse for anyone?

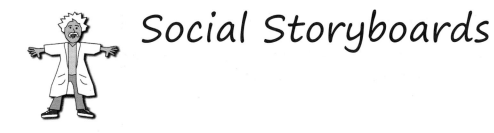

Social Storyboards

It's all about helping you to succeed

Social Storyboards are a great way to help you picture yourself in a situation you may be anxious about.

By using words and pictures in a comic strip format and building it together with family and friends, you can feel confident that you'll reach your goal.

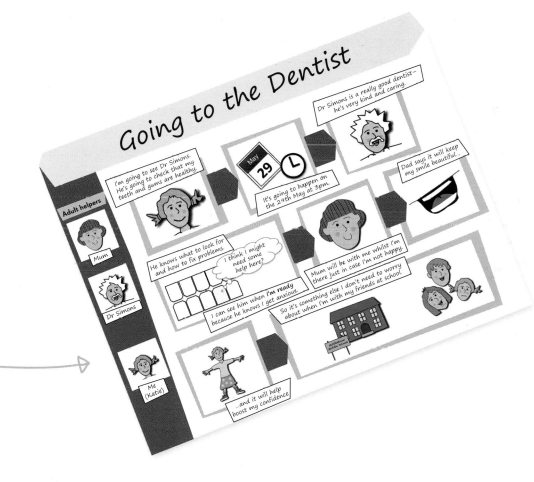

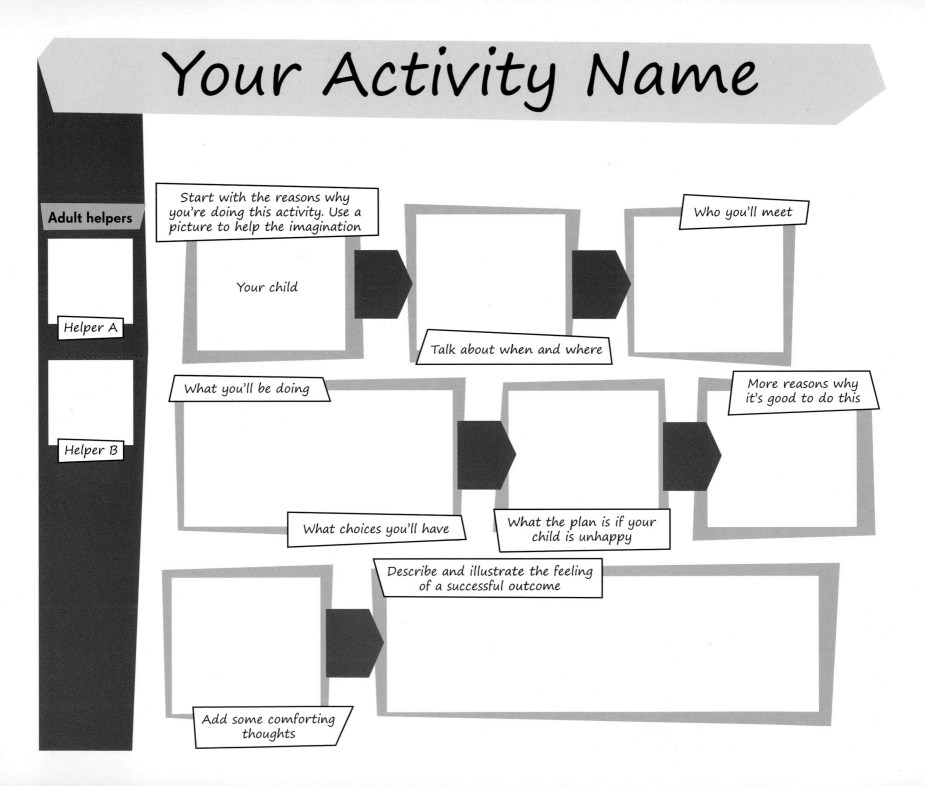

Your Activity Name

Adult helpers

Helper A

Helper B

Start with the reasons why you're doing this activity. Use a picture to help the imagination

Your child

Who you'll meet

Talk about when and where

What you'll be doing

More reasons why it's good to do this

What choices you'll have

What the plan is if your child is unhappy

Describe and illustrate the feeling of a successful outcome

Add some comforting thoughts

Going to the Dentist

Here is a cartoon example, but using photographs is a great way to help it feel more real and personal. You can build up a stock of pictures and use them over and over again.

Adult helpers

Mum

Dr Simons

Me (Katie)

I'm going to see Dr Simons. He's going to check that my teeth and gums are healthy.

It's going to happen on the 29th May at 3pm.

Dr Simons is a really good dentist— he's very kind and caring.

He knows what to look for and how to fix problems.

I think I might need some help here?

I can see him when **I'm ready** because he knows I get anxious.

Mum will be with me whilst I'm there just in case I'm not happy.

Dad says it will keep my smile beautiful...

So it's something else I don't need to worry about when I'm with my friends at school.

...and it will help boost my confidence

Inner Intelligence: Things that Drive Us

In addition to our emotions there are other things that drive who we are and what we do:

★ *Ambition* – things we want to achieve (our goals and dreams).

★ *Desire* – things we want for ourselves and the people we care about.

★ *Experience* – what we've learned from the past, and how it shapes our future.

Here are some ideas that will help you get the very best out of life. You may already be doing some of them...

Find the thing that inspires you

Everyone has something they enjoy doing and find rewarding.

Sometimes you don't always find it straight away, or your first encounter wasn't a particularly encouraging experience. But finding what inspires you is really important. It will help you to understand what's important to you, where you want to go in life and what you want to do.

It could be science, sport, writing, art or something else. It's the passion you feel about doing something you enjoy.

It's often the case that to do great work, is to love what you do. This simple idea will help you both at school and well into your adult life.

Be a great problem solver

This may surprise you, but one of the reasons the human race is so successful is because we have learnt to become the world's best problem solvers. This ability is quite literally in our genes. But sometimes if you try a solve too many problems at once, it gets tiring.

1. It's often useful to write your problems down in a list. This takes the weight off your mind and allows you to clear your head.

2. You can then use this list to prioritise what's important to do now and what to attempt later. This is really important because if you try to do too many things at once, you often end up doing none of them.

3. The final step is the hardest: figuring out the solution. But interestingly the solution often comes from looking at the sources of the problem – how and when things came together to make the problem happen in the first place.

Don't be surprised to learn that one of the things you may need to change to make things better is something about yourself or your approach.

Learn to be flexible

The gifts of wisdom can often come from unexpected places, so accepting that everyone has something to offer will help you respect them and, in turn, over time, gain their respect too.

A great way to be flexible is to try something different, or do something a different way. Even if you end up not liking it, provided that it's not dangerous, at least you've had a new learning experience.

Outer Intelligence: Understanding Other People

Don't worry if you sometimes feel you do not always understand other people.

Everyone is different, so you need to find a balance of mutual acceptance.

This balance point will be different for different people.

Watch out for the signs

Very few people escape through life without some kind of trauma at some point in their lives. It's part of being human.

Everyone deals with extreme stress differently. So even if you find it hard to imagine what it's like to be someone in their position, it's important to give them time and space to deal with their difficulties.

Angry
Please stand clear

Disappointed
Enter with caution

Sad
Understanding only beyond this point

Balance how you feel about someone

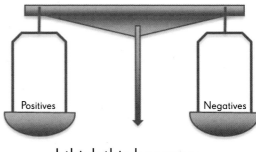

Positives   Negatives

I think this because...

Get a second opinion...or even a third or fourth. If you are not sure about someone or something, there is never any harm in getting another opinion from people whose judgement you already trust. Indeed, the fact that they may see things differently may be useful.

But remember not to get cross with them if they don't agree with you. It's about getting a balanced view, and that can only be achieved by weighing up more than one opinion.

Get angry, but don't get even

You cannot make something right, by doing something wrong

This is a fundamental and universal law of Nature.

It's often difficult to quell the thirst for revenge when someone makes you very angry. But attempting to get even is likely to put you into the 'Loop of Doom'.

You upset me

The Loop of Doom

I'll upset you

The 'Loop of Doom' is a place of mutually assured disruption where nobody wins and everyone loses. Satisfaction is short term, often followed by yet more anger, and so the cycle or loop continues.

To break free of the loop *you* have to change the way you feel about what has happened, and change your response to it. Generally, substituting something positive for something negative is a good place to start. A gesture of reconciliation, forgiveness or an offer to not retaliate shows that you have the greater strength of character and maturity.

What about people I'm not sure about?

People can often surprise and delight you, but they can often let you down too. It's less about what they do over a single incident, more about what they do over several of them. You often hear people say 'Don't judge me', but in truth all of us are judged by our words and deeds by everyone around us, every day. People's judgments are often based on things like caring, honesty, intelligence and other signs of character.

Congruence is when people do what they say. It does not guarantee that they will be nice or a good choice of friend, but they will at least be more predictable than those who lack it.

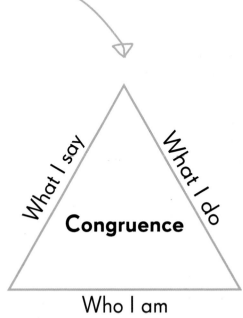

What I say

What I do

Congruence

Who I am

Joining the Digital Dots

It's all about having fun, learning and being safe

Welcome to the world of interpersonal communications

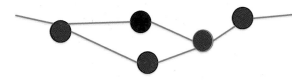

Perfected over the last 100 years, what you will learn will allow you to expand your knowledge, communicate with others and have fun safely.

Networking, sharing, collaborating and communicating with others is exactly what the internet and communication devices were designed for.

But just like the real world, the virtual world has dangers too.

Safety and security start with knowing about who and what you can trust.

So let's begin.

Social Media: A Good Place to Start is with What You Know

Think about the *people* you know and trust.

Are the people you know in your circles of friendship reliable and trustworthy?

Do you feel they have your best interests at heart?

Are they fun to share ideas with, or do you have reservations about who else might be in their communication network?

Relationship networks

Just like in the real world, in the virtual world direct relationships are the ones you are most likely to know more about.

The further you get away from direct knowledge, the greater the risks to you.

There is no harm in being cautious about people until you know more about them.

In general, unless you've met them, by definition you don't really know much about them. This is especially true of friends of friends.

Not sure

Unknown

Unknown

OK

OK

Me

Circles of friendship

Being a 'gatekeeper of your heart' is all about ensuring only the people you really trust get close to it.

The closer people get, the more they need to prove to you their honesty and integrity.

Only people you are truly sure about and really trust should get beyond the inner circle.

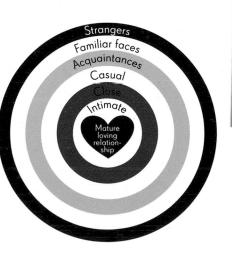

Strangers
Familiar faces
Acquaintances
Casual
Close
Intimate
Mature loving relation-ship

Generally it's not a good idea to use social media when you are angry or upset — just like shouting something out in a large crowded room, you may later regret what you have said.

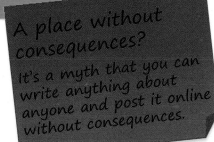

A place without consequences?

It's a myth that you can write anything about anyone and post it online without consequences.

Using the Internet: What 'Free' on the Internet Really Means

Many people think that most things on the internet are free. Unfortunately that is seldom if ever true. What's being sold is information about *you*.

When you sign up for a 'free' service, the service provider will try and gather as much information about you as they can, to use it to sell you things later, or to sell to others. So be careful what personal information you allow to escape onto the internet. Because *once it's released it's impossible to get back*.

Volunteering information

Be careful what you sign up for. Ensure you give only basic information about yourself.

In general you should avoid giving details about your age, sex, location or personal circumstances.

If a service asks you for this type of information, always complete it with a parent or carer.

Some services are age restricted. This may be for a very good reason.

Phishing

'YOU NEED TO TAKE IMMEDIATE ACTION in order to prevent you from having to...'

Some people and organisations will get hold of a list of email addresses and send out emails in the hope that some will respond.

They can pretend to be a bank, an important internet security feature or anything that may scare people into taking action and parting with money or information (theirs or other people's).

Before you respond to *any* request like this, ask yourself 'Is it real?' and 'Why would they need this information?'

Celebrity searches

Every year a new celebrity is named 'the most dangerous celebrity to search for on the web' by leading online security companies.

Cyber criminals will often use the names of popular celebrities to lure people to websites that have malicious software. So always make sure your computer's security software is up-to-date.

Mobile Devices: Power in Your Pocket

Although small in size, mobile devices are pretty powerful tools.

If you hold a lot of personal information in your mobile, it's important that you protect it well. Make sure you are always aware of where you leave it when you're not using it, and add a password so people can't log onto it without your knowledge. It's also a good idea to adjust the settings so that people you don't know can't send you emails or texts.

As a general rule it's best only to communicate electronically with people you've met in the real world. Be suspicious of people who hide behind a cyber identity only.

Cyberbullying

A dispute, argument or dislike can often spill over into the cyber world with what might be considered nasty or malicious email and text messages. It's important to notify your parents/carers or teachers of this type of conduct, as well as to refrain from it yourself.

No matter how angry or upset anyone may feel, you can never make something good by doing something that is wrong.

Password protection

★ Always protect the access to your device with a password, and a short duration auto-lock.

★ Never share or tell your password to anyone who is not in your inner circle.

★ Never email or text your password details or leave them as a voicemail message.

Protecting you and your device

★ Don't text or email while walking or cycling.

★ Never leave your device lying around in a public area or an area strangers may have access to.

★ If your device has a location tracker, ensure only people you want to know have access to your location.

Your Digital Footprint: What Goes Online, Stays Online

In the real world your reputation will become your biggest asset, so make sure you don't do anything in the virtual world to damage it.

Does it really matter what I say?

In the same way as in the real world, you cannot simply say what you think online or via text. In many ways you need to be more careful, simply because what you do and say can catch up with you later and be played back to you, your peers, and those you care about – sometimes not in the context in which it was intended.

The simple rule of not saying anything you would not like said about yourself is the best guide here.

This rule applies even if your online profile hides your true identity. It's a myth that hiding who you are is a guarantee of anonymity.

Using privacy tools

If you are using social media there are some simple things you can do to keep your activities away from anyone who is not the intended audience.

★ *Directory information* – make sure only those you want to can see your picture, your name and profile information.

★ *Sharing* – ensure that only those you want to see your status updates, what you are doing now and postings, can see them.

★ *Application, games and website sharing filters* – these control what information is shared with organisations outside your group, including search engines.

★ *Block list* – this is good for blocking invitations from people you do not know.

Do I care what other people think?

As you get older you do indeed care more and more about what other people think.

You may want to be seen as funny, clever, popular or cool as part of your real-life reputation, but your online one is every bit as important, so take care to protect it.

Creating your own digital content is a great way of expressing yourself and interacting with the people who really matter to you. But you need to be careful about publishing information about yourself.

In general, it's a good idea not to publish anything that could be misinterpreted as offensive, rude, or inappropriate.

What might have seemed like a good idea at the time might not seem so a few days, months or even years from now.

Virtual Worlds, Multiplayer Games, Chat Rooms and Webcams
Interacting with Stangers Online

It can be great fun interacting with people who seem to share the same interests as you do, so long as you stick to some simple rules.

Using your webcam

Only use it to chat with people you already know. Don't let a complete stranger or someone you've known online for a while convince you otherwise.

Don't be secretive with your parents or carer

If your online friend has asked you not to speak to anyone else about them, this is a sure sign that they have something to hide.

Talking to an adult in your family about new online friends is a great way to sense-check how you feel about someone and their behaviour towards you.

Be more cautious with friends you've only ever met online

Don't share pictures, information or facts about you, your family and friends with people you've never met in the real world.

Inappropriate, Harmful and Illegal Content

Being curious is part of growing up, and learning about the world. But in the virtual world there are few (if any) rules, so you have to apply some of your own to stay safe.

Use the same principles as for film and TV

Age limits and viewing times are set up to protect kids from seeing harmful and inappropriate material. Web browser controls and safe search tools help protect you from seeing disturbing content. It's there to protect you.

Don't click on links from people you don't know

Without knowing the person who sent you the link, it's impossible to guess what might be waiting for you at the other end of it.

Since the majority of unsolicited internet emails lead to inappropriate content or malicious websites, these emails are best deleted.

Copyright and illegal downloading

It's always nice to get something for free, but downloading or sharing movies, music and written material you know are not free is stealing, and it's a criminal offence.

Digital Safety Contract

Openness and trust are the basis of every meaningful relationship, so why not sign up to a symbol of that trust with your own parent/carer with a Digital Safety Contract?

Parent and Child Digital Safety Contract

1. In order for my child to use the important resources of digital technology, it is my duty as a parent or carer to keep them safe and secure at all times. To do this I *must*:

   a. know the websites and services that they use

   b. know the names and usernames of online friends they have that I have not met in person

   c. know the passwords of communication enabled devices which I undertake only to use in a emergency and never divulge to anyone, including family or friends.

2. We will talk openly about our internet and mobile communication activities and avoid any type of hostile online activity of any kind.

3. We'll use blocks and filters to protect ourselves from inappropriate material, and ensure any downloaded material does not infringe copyright and is not immoral or degrading in any way.

4. When flagrant and repeated abuses of this mutual agreement are apparent, we both accept that this cannot be allowed to continue, so the right of access will need to be modified.

5. We both undertake that it is our duty to report any inappropriate, dangerous or harmful digital or real world behaviour to the school, college or local law enforcement department.

We the undersigned agree to the above terms and conditions.

Child's signature: _____

Parent or carer's signature: _____   Date: _ _ / _ _ / _ _

Refresh and Renewal

It's wonderful having parents, carers and friends to listen and help you with these problems. But in the same way that you need time to rest and recover, your helpers need it too so that they are refreshed to help you again and again. Why not suggest they take a short break, and do something relaxing or sporty to help them recharge their emotional and problem-solving batteries?

Remember you are a team, and team members look after each other.